HOW IS IT THAT WE LIVE

or

SHAKEY JAKE + ALICE

Len Jenkin

BROADWAY PLAY PUBLISHING INC
New York
www.broadwayplaypublishing.com
info@broadwayplaypublishing.com

Cover art: detail from *Dante's Inferno*, Len Jenkin,
acrylic on canvas, 2015

First edition: May 2019
I S B N: 978-0-88145-831-2

Book design: Marie Donovan
Page make-up: Adobe InDesign
Typeface: Palatino

HOW IS IT THAT WE LIVE or SHAKEY JAKE +
ALICE was first produced at the Undermain Theater
in Dallas, opening on 16 September 2018. The cast and
creative contributors were:

SHAKEY JAKE .... Jim Jorgensen
ALICE ....Shannon Kearns
SPEAKER ONE, CLARENCE NIGHTINGALE,
SWEET LUCY .... Bruce Dubose
SPEAKER TWO, SNAKEHIPS,
LITTLE SISTER .... Danielle Georgiou

Director ....Katherine Owens
Set, Lights, Costumes design .... John Arnone

SETTING & CHARACTERS

I. *Under The Bridge*

SHAKEY JAKE
ALICE
CLARENCE NIGHTINGALE
EVANGELINE, *who isn't there*

II. A *House On The River*

SHAKEY JAKE
ALICE
SWEET LUCY (*aka* CLARENCE NIGHTINGALE)
SNAKE HIPS (*aka* EVANGELINE)

III. *At The Bone Orchard*

SHAKEY JAKE
ALICE
LITTLE SISTER (*aka* SNAKE HIPS/EVANGELINE)
SWEET LUCY (*aka* CLARENCE NIGHTINGALE), *who isn't
    there*

NOTE

There are two couples.

ALICE *and* JAKE *are the same age, and they grow older from scene to scene as we go on.*

CLARENCE NIGHTINGALE/SWEET LUCY *and* EVANGELINE/SNAKE HIPS/LITTLE SISTER *are an older man and a young woman.*

They never age.

When one of these four people isn't speaking directly to each other, there is descriptive language.

This is always spoken by CLARENCE, *or* EVANGELINE, *or a mix of the two. This talk is marked* SPEAKER, *to leave open to discovery who best to say those words.*

MUSIC

The music indicated in this text is meant to be suggestive. Different music, or more music, or less music, can be used, depending on the style and needs of any individual production. How the music is used (as underscoring, length, etc.) can also certainly vary. This music outside the dialogue can be tracks, or performed by the cast and/or an onstage band, or any combination of the two.

The music within the text (Little Birdy and the blues songs) should not be changed.

ADDITIONAL NOTE ON MUSIC

For performance of copyrighted songs, arrangements
or recordings referenced in this play, permission
of the copyright owner(s) must be obtained. Other
songs, arrangements or recordings may be substituted
provided permission from the copyright owner(s) of
such songs, arrangements or recordings is obtained
or songs, arrangements or recordings in the public
domain may be substituted.

Shadows we are, and like shadows, we depart
—**from a sundial**

For Ramona

I. UNDER THE BRIDGE

SPEAKER:
In these times of ours
though concerning the exact year there is no need to be
precise
two figures shelter under an arch of concrete and steel
River Road Bridge
thunder, the crack/flash of lightning
warm rain
traffic overhead
wind and water
Shakey Jake and Alice
the two of them
summer evening closing in

SPEAKER:
Jakey's got his car parked under there
'68 Cadillac Coupe de Ville
Candyapple red
suicide knob's an eightball

SPEAKER:
Alice steps out into the rain
face up, arms wide, mouth open

SPEAKER:
Drinking raindrops

JAKE:
Alice, you're getting soaked

ALICE:
I'm not made of sugar, Jakey

JAKE:
Your mom's gonna ask me how
I let you get caught out in a fucking thunderstorm

ALICE:
I won't melt away

JAKE:
Lightning's gonna fry you

ALICE:
I love it

JAKE:
Dead Alice

ALICE:
I love it

JAKE:
Me, too
your hair dripping down
wet shirt on your skin
the way your back curves down into your butt

ALICE:
I meant the rain

JAKE:
You in it
Come back under here
I got a clean rag in the car

SPEAKER:
And Alice dries her face, her hair…

SPEAKER:
Under a row of hedges close by
a weasel hides from the rain
touches his nose to the paper thin shell of a cricket
nothing left inside
sang itself utterly away

ALICE:
We stay here long enough, something's gonna happen

JAKE:
Something's always happening
It can't help it

ALICE:
I don't mean the world turning round
I mean something

JAKE:
What?

ALICE:
I don't know

SPEAKER:
Alice's hair's dirty blonde
pale skin
Up close you see the thin blue veins in her hands
in her neck
She was co-captain of the cheerleading squad at their
high school
and you could tell

ALICE:
Be aggressive, be aggressive
B E, A G G R E S S I V E
Go team!
So utterly stupid
I quit

SPEAKER:
Flicker of passing headlights from the road above
a siren and fading

JAKE:
Alice?

ALICE:
What is it, Jakey?

JAKE:
My Dad's worse
emphysema's bad, and he's still smoking
He sneaks 'em Camel straights carton hid in his sock
drawer
My Mom's gotta nag him to do his breathing exercises
he's so weak some days she can't go to work at Sears
keeps up they'll fire her

ALICE:
That's hard, Jakey
hard for them, hard for you

JAKE:
I lie in bed at night, wait to hear the next coughing fit
like to shake the house down
It's fucking extraordinary actually

ALICE:
What?

JAKE:
Them
how they hold each other up in this world
and after all the shit I've done, suspended from school
twice
getting arrested that time
they still care about me

ALICE:
That's cause you're a loveable delinquent

JAKE:
No it's not and I'm not
It's just the way it is with them

ALICE:
They love you, that's all

JAKE:
They're sweetheart drunks
Love and tears come easy

ALICE:
Some parents take the kids, put 'em in a bag
drown 'em in the river like kittens
You're a fortunate son, Jakey

JAKE:
Maybe I am

ALICE:
I come from a long line of losers
Uncle Aaron, my Mom's baby brother
crazy as a goose
tried to rob a Quik-Stop with a twelve gauge
killed the cashier by accident, girl still in high school
he's in jail probably die there
My mom's the only one who visits the sonofabitch
She hates you, you know

JAKE:
Who?

ALICE:
My Mom
hates you energetically

JAKE:
Why? How come? I'm...

ALICE:
Cause I'm not home right now
cause I'm under this bridge in the rain
They want me to be happy

JAKE:
They don't think I make you happy?

ALICE:
Nope
and they're right

JAKE:
Come on Alice don't say that shit

ALICE:
You mix me up and make me crazy
make me forget everyone else
everything else
but you don't make me happy, Jakey

JAKE:
I'm not gonna understand you, am I, Alice?

ALICE:
That's okay, Shakey Jakey
that's not your job
That's my job
However, that all doesn't mean a thing, as I don't love
you
the way I love Bobby Darin
(Sings)
Dream lover, where are you

JAKE:
Bobby Darin's gay

ALICE:
No he's not

JAKE:
How do you know?

ALICE:
I just do.

SPEAKER:
Thunder
wind and rain
not letting up
not yet
Jakey's given name was Jacob, after the ladder and his
grandpa
His mom's dad
Who smoked Chesterfields, drank Canadian Club
boatswain's mate on destroyers

fought the Japs at Guadalcanal, came back in one
piece...

JAKE:
Torpedoed three times, saved once by a dolphin
once by a mermaid
once by Jesus H Christ
At his funeral my grandma threw herself into his grave

ALICE:
She did that?

JAKE:
No lie
She didn't want to let him go
Took two gravediggers to drag her out
You know something, Alice?
You make me pretty damn happy

ALICE:
No, I don't
not all by myself
You help
You know what I am, Jakey?
A thing in your head
I fit onto a map you got in there
clay into a ready mold
So you love me
Right now, anyway
under the River Road Bridge

JAKE:
Clever girl, Alice
But you got that one wrong
You're not my echo of something
Or someone
Only you

SPEAKER:
And Jakey jumps into his Coupe de Ville
He kicks on the radio

JAKE:
Ooo poppa doo
How do you do
It's Shakey Jake, ladies, and I'm on the scene
Cruising the night with my sound machine

SPEAKER:
Delco speakers bass booster
and the music bounces
off the concrete

SPEAKER:
And Alice dances
in the rain smeared headlights

(Vision of ALICE)

(Suggested music: The Tide Is High [Paragons])

SPEAKER:
Shakey Jake dances with her
The fat moon breaks loose, spins off down the sky
Alice jumps up onto Jake, wraps her legs around him
kisses him
slick with sweat and rain
Jakey tries to keep his balance holding up their two
bodies
and a man comes out of the dark

CLARENCE:
Evangeline!

SPEAKER:
One leg in a muddy boot
other leg cut off right above the knee, pants knotted up
at the stump

CLARENCE:
Aluminium crutch

SPEAKER:
long red coat

soaking wet bogeyman
shakes himself like a dog

JAKE:
Uh, Mister...

CLARENCE:
Nightingale, at your service

JAKE:
private party
Get outta here Mister Nightingale

CLARENCE:
They call me Clarence
You see me!

SPEAKER #2:
Thunder rolls again, soft at first
From beyond the hills
then close
Lightning and rain

CLARENCE:
I go back out there in the wet I'll get the arthuritis
leave me hoppin' with a double twist
Your damn fault, be in hell with the wicked

ALICE:
Can't we let him stay till the rain...

CLARENCE:
Don't need you to fight for me, Alice
I'm as much a man as Jakey over there, limbered up,
lubricated
brain ticking over like a cheap watch
I'm ahead of the play

JAKE:
How do you know our names?

CLARENCE:
Everybody around here knows Shakey Jake and Alice

JAKE:
You from around here?

CLARENCE:
Course I am
born and raised in this briarpatch

JAKE:
This is our place, me and Alice
I still want you gone

CLARENCE:
Jakey, have pity on the working man
I had steady employment
doorman of distinction at the Palace of the Czar
six in the pm to the midnite hour
They fired me, damn Russki hoodlum bastards from
Kraznopoloski
Howsumever, I stole my doorman coat
You see it!
Right on my back!
Coat of a Cossack! Epaulets!
Grab the golden doorknob
open the golden door
Velcome! Bon soir, bon soir
velcome to the Palace of the Czar
have the beautiful evening, Mademoiselle
Average night three hundred bucks in tips
do the math, kids
Me and Evangeline were living large
Evangeline! Evangeline!
I gotta admit the happy couple has been sleeping
rough lately
gas station bathrooms
Sunoco right up the River Road
I got a Hills Brothers coffee can to cook in
the red one with the man in the dress
Handful of pebbles
Shake one time, shake two times

Shake it three!
Rain on the roof
You got ears?
Rain in the can, rain in the world!

SPEAKER:
As below, so above
The rain blows wilder than ever
coming down in sheets

CLARENCE:
(Sings)

O Evangelina, don't you cry for me
I come from Diddy Wah Diddy
With a banjo on my knee
Rained all night the day I left
Weather it was dry...

SPEAKER:
And Clarence pauses
Silence
Far off a dog howls
Silence once more
Clarence listens for something, but he can't hear it
Not yet

CLARENCE:
What's that vehicle you got there, Jakey?

JAKE:
Cadillac

CLARENCE:
Ragtop

Coup de Ville Cadillac, Coup de Ville

JAKE:
Sixty-eight

CLARENCE:
Burn the wind, baby

And who's this woman you got here, Jakey?
Zat chick too young to fry?
She a devil or an angel?

JAKE:
Alice is an angel

CLARENCE:
Can she turn back the waters?

JAKE:
She's a high school graduate angel first in her class

CLARENCE:
Save us from the flood to come?

JAKE:
Off to college Angel Alice!

ALICE:
I can change all this rainwater into wine
red as blood twelve percent alcohol

CLARENCE:
Whoa, don't lie to me, Alice
You're no angel

JAKE:
Angel to me

CLARENCE:
That's different
It's one thing to fuck somebody righteously
and wipe away a tear or two
No small thing in this world
specially if you look like one of those Dallas Cowboys
Cheerleaders
Those are All-American ladies
I've done it myself, and I'm no saint

ALICE:
Done what?

CLARENCE:
Given comfort in the long night
the one where the hands of the clock stop
between ticks
Tick
And you can wait for the tock
till Kingdom Come
The bird of the long night that's me
Come on over babies, underneath my wing
You got some soda pop?

JAKE:
You want a beer?

CLARENCE:
Delighted
though I'm usually abstemious
Nobody at all

SPEAKER:
And Jakey goes to his car and pulls three cold ones
out of the cooler

JAKE:
Beers all around

CLARENCE:
Here's to you both

SPEAKER:
And all three drink
Quite the little party
Under the River Road Bridge
I think I'll have one myself…

CLARENCE:
Sometime back
night in America
I'm blind as a mole
groping my way down Central Avenue
tapping side to side with my redtip walking stick

trying to find the Ramona Hotel, where I have a room
third floor front number six brass feel it on the door
Evangeline runs off on me again
bitch grabs my poke and disappears
Then snow comes on, falling thick and fast
I can feel it wet on my face
Sharp wind
I cry for help but no one hears me in the snow and
darkness
I stumble into an alley out of the storm
fall down and sleep, and the drifting snow covers me
Stray dog sniffs, touches his wet nose to my cold cheek
When they find me in the morning I'm stone dead
Someone had stolen my walking stick

ALICE:
You're not dead

JAKE:
You're not blind

CLARENCE:
That was another time
People change

SPEAKER:
Silence
Truck horn, as an eighteen wheeler rolls by above
Silence
Clarence listens for something, but he can't hear it
Not yet

CLARENCE:
EVANGELINE!
Come outta the damn woods
you oughta see these kids
They're all right!
EVANGELINE!
She's up in the trees with the rackety raccoons
I don't hardly see her anymore

She's a wild thing
She makes my heart sing
She makes everything...groovy!
My Evangeline's gonna get raccoon bit and die back
there in the woods
She'd do better looking into ponds, see her own face
In the green mirror
God's beautiful creatures...
always hungry, and some of them have teeth
Beware of snappers!
One of those bastards took my pinky to the bottom of
the well
Hammerheaded shark took my leg off, right above the
knee
I carved a pegleg from a sycamore
then one midnite in the woods, moon playing tricks in
the trees
like a fool I fell asleep by a pond
That leg was eaten right off me
Beavers
God's creatures are welcome to the pieces of me they
need
Thus, parts of me are elsewhere
My heart's in the forest with Evangeline

It's all right
Not a worry in the world
She comes back to me every time
Eventually
Evangeline!
We gotta go now

JAKE:
Where you going?

CLARENCE:
Zat your business?

ALICE:
It's the night-time
Decent people in bed already

CLARENCE:
We have an engagement, me and Evangeline
with the Queen of Sheba
She's gonna pass by tonight, with all her servants,
on her way to the moon
Her cupbearer rides right next to her on a white horse
He pours her a clean shot of Remy whenever she raises
her little finger
Tell you the truth kids
It's hard for me
to go on without her
I'm heading over that hill
If I can make it to the top, the road down ain't nothing
at all
You see Evangeline, tell her which way I went

ALICE:
How will we know her?

CLARENCE:
Oh, you'll know her
Tell her Clarence Nightingale loves her still
Keep your hands out of other people's pockets
Don't rob no liquor stores
Look into Alice's eyes, Jakey
like falling down a wishing well
Ain't it, Alice?
Au revoir, mademoiselle, au revoir
Door's over that hill
the golden door
I can open it
I'm the doorman

SPEAKER:
And he's gone, and from a great distance
halfway around the world

CLARENCE:
Wop bobalooma balop bop bop
Tutti frutti
All rootie!

SPEAKER:
And from an even greater distance
beyond the Milky Way

CLARENCE:
Evangeline! Evangeline….

JAKE:
Man o man
Who the hell was that?
Made me nervous
fucking know-it-all
running his mouth at people under the bridge
who gave him shelter from the storm

ALICE:
Blind man in a blizzard
stumbling down the avenue
You think that's how we live?
Who we are?

JAKE:
Just a story

ALICE:
There are truer ones

JAKE:
You didn't like him much

ALICE:
Au contraire, Shakey-jakey
He's just my kind of sonofabitch
Like you

SPEAKER:
From under the arch of concrete and steel
Jake steps out, looks up
rain's let up
clouds coming apart
there's a piece of the night sky

JAKE:
The hangman's daughter

ALICE:
What?

JAKE:
You

ALICE:
My dad's not a hangman

JAKE:
I like calling you that
cause of the animal in your eyes
I do believe it's a fox in there

ALICE:
Is that a compliment, Jakey?

JAKE:
Could be

ALICE:
My father's a funeral director
mortician, with a license
He's a very gentle man, Jakey,
not a hangman
When I was ten years old he put me to work in the
business
so I would get familiar with death, he said, and love
my life the more
He gave me a basket of gardenias and a handful of
safety pins
and I went downstairs to the cold room

flowers for dead men
After a few weeks I told him I had too much
homework
couldn't do it anymore

JAKE:
Were you scared of the bodies?

ALICE:
Empty shells
The smell of formaldehyde and methanol was giving
me headaches

JAKE:
You know what, Alice?

ALICE:
What, Jakey?

JAKE:
Fuck Harvard

ALICE:
Don't be like that
you're wound up tighter than a cheap watch
you've got to lay it down, Jakey
Let it go
They don't lock me in those dorms
You can visit me

JAKE:
That doesn't change anything
You're leaving me, Alice

ALICE:
No I'm not

JAKE:
You damn well are

ALICE:
I have got to live my life

JAKE:
What are you doing right now?
Under the River Road Bridge
Dying?

ALICE:
That, too

JAKE:
You know something, Alice?
In your own sweet way, you're a bitch

ALICE:
Stop it, Jakey
Please
You're making me cry

JAKE:
You're the one who's leaving

ALICE:
What am I supposed to do?
Live in a cage in your basement?
Why don't you beat me to death with a tree branch,
show me how much you love me?
Drag me into the woods
cover me over with leaves
Better, come up to Harvard
drag me outta the dorm
beat me to death and throw my body in the River
Charles
let it carry me down to Boston Bay

JAKE:
I wont have time
for all that beating and dragging
I'll be in China

ALICE:
What?

JAKE:
You're going deaf, Alice. And so young.

ALICE:
If you go to China, who's gonna take care of your Mom
and Dad?

JAKE:
God
God'll do it
I don't care
I'm gonna be a Buddhist, write poems on trees
They're waiting for me at the Lotus Temple, on the
Sacred Mountain of Jade
Tigers guard the gates

ALICE:
My mom's a Buddhist

JAKE:
Your mom's a nutcase

ALICE:
That, too
You don't even know what a Buddhist is

JAKE:
Someone who believes
this world is a place of suffering
but if we knew ourselves, what we truly are
we'd know its not like it seems
under this bridge, in this town, on the green ball

ALICE:
Man is born to sorrow as the sparks fly upward

JAKE:
Where'd you hear that?

ALICE:
In church last Sunday

JAKE:
Church full of Buddhists

ALICE:
Maybe so

JAKE:
I can't be hanging around sipping white wine in the
Harvard Yard
waiting for you to get outta class
I'll be out where the Chinese moon meets the Yellow
River
I'll send you postcards, pictures of the Green Lama
pots of tea

ALICE:
I hate you
You're making fun of me

JAKE:
You're the one who's leaving

ALICE:
You don't get it yet, do you, Jakey
I'm your girl
Now and forever
I'm your girl

JAKE:
I'll visit

ALICE:
Promise me

JAKE:
I promise, Alice
Cross my heart and hope to die

ALICE:
Look, Jakey

JAKE:
Look at what?

ALICE:
If we stayed here long enough, something had to
happen

JAKE:
What had to happen?

ALICE:
Look
Rainbow in the dark

JAKE:
I can't see it

ALICE:
I can't see it either, but I know its there
I can see its arc
across the stars
Will you remember me, Jakey?

JAKE:
You mean tomorrow?
Next week? Next year…

ALICE:
I mean remember me
in the smoke
of all your days and nights
on your deathbed
angel of death at your feet and some gray-haired old
lady is holding your hand
and she sees your eyes open wide
only you don't see anything
not anymore
On that dime, will you remember me?

JAKE:
I don't plan on dying

ALICE:
Death has no mercy

not even on your skinny ass
Answer the question

JAKE:
I don't know, Alice
I truly don't
I hope so, but I don't know

ALICE:
I'll remember you

JAKE:
How do you know that?
You're eighteen
You could live a long life
get married, have children, lovers
Shakey Jakey will be a long time gone

ALICE:
No
I'll remember you
last thing before the lights go out
your face

SPEAKER:
They hold each other
Shakey Jake and Alice

(*Lights shift to hold this final image*)

(*Scene out*)

II. A HOUSE ON THE RIVER

SPEAKER:
Years later
Alice's house by the river
late December
not a cloud in the evening sky
all still in heaven and earth
the Milky Way

SPEAKER:
Shakey Jake on the road
back in America
Hitch-hiking
Boarded up storefronts
Wagon Wheel Tavern
Three Wise Men Asian Café
Papa John's Take and Bake
Sunoco, and out along the two-lane heading out of
town
rusted playgrounds Walmart superstore Los Rojos Bar
Solid Gold Gentleman's Club

JAKE:
Hi Hat Liquors
Taco Palace
and a long empty stretch of scrub
walk through America
Scrapper Blackwell and Yank Rachell down on the
corner
In front of the liquor store
intersection of the highway and the moon…
Old Harmony Silvertone and a mandolin
How long, how long, has that evening train been gone
how long how long baby how long…
I lie awake in this bedroll
can't stop the tears wet on my cheek
taste of salt
They say even a prisoner in his cell
a child lost in the woods
can find the way home
Why not me?

(Vision of JAKE*)*

(Suggested music—Little Rain Falling *[Jimmy Reed])*

SPEAKER:
Jakey sent a letter to Alice's parent's house a year ago

Her mother brought it over, stuck the envelope under
Alice's front door

ALICE:
Return address Soto Cano Air Base, Comayagua,
Honduras
Now my child is asleep
Unfold the letter once more
read it by the candle, over and over
The flame is low, dawn not yet come
candle flickers out

SPEAKER:
Alice sits in the dark
listening to a loose coupler chain driven by the wind
clangs again and again on the side of a boxcar
left to rust on a siding in the woods nearby
Before sunrise
frost in the churchyard
grass white around the gravestones
half erased by time

SPEAKER:
Sunoco station
Pay phone by the men's room
Jakey makes a call

JAKE:
Sorry to bother you ma'am
I'm looking for Alice?

SPEAKER: (As ALICE's mother)
You find her, tell her she owes her loving mother
six hundred twenty bucks
two months back rent, August-September before she
found her own place
It's almost merry goddamn Christmas
Hold on while I fire up this Chesterfield…

JAKE:
I'm holding

SPEAKER: *(As* ALICE's *mother)*
This is Shakey-Jakey, isn't it?

JAKE:
That's me
I went to high school with Alice

SPEAKER: *(As* ALICE's *mother)*
I know damn well who you are

SPEAKER:
And a silence as Mom thinks it over...

SPEAKER: *(As* ALICE's *mother)*
Alice lives right here, crosstown
on the River Road

JAKE:
Thanks, thanks for telling me

SPEAKER: *(As* ALICE's *mother)*
Red house I forget the number
screendoor's got some Christmas lights, twinkly
You know something, Jakey?
You're lucky all she took was your heart

JAKE:
What's that supposed to mean?

SPEAKER: *(As* ALICE's *mother)*
Fuck off, Jakey
You and Alice can go to hell

SPEAKER:
Alice sits at her kitchen table
trying once more to write a letter in reply

ALICE:
Trying to explain herself
to tell him
how she is

SPEAKER:
She can't write one word

SPEAKER:
Caw! Caw! Caw!

SPEAKER:
The cries come through the open window with its
yellow curtains
and they wake her child

ALICE:
Hush! Be still
back to sleep…
It's just the moonlight
makes the crows cry so
all night long

SPEAKER:
At last her baby sleeps
the crows sing a lullaby in his dreams
She takes up her pen, and thinks of Shakey Jake
U S Army soldier in Honduras
In Alice's kitchen, teardrops mark the page

SPEAKER:
First violet line on the horizon
Woods by the railyards
home to chipmunks, field mice
and the hawks that feed on them
Who's that shivering in the pre-dawn dark
trying to start a fire with sticks soaked in dew?
A spark takes—see who it is by the glow of that tiny
fire
Shakey-Jakey, a regular boy scout

JAKE:
Lemme make up one of my patented poorboy
speedballs—
four tablespoons of Nescafe, shot of hot water
fill with bourbon and stir
Drink up, Jakey, miles to go
Ahhhh!

Light in the east, beyond the hills
crash of switchers shuffling boxcars in the yards
fucking cold
It's so cold in China, the birds can't hardly sing
So cold in China, the birds can't hardly sing
That woman of mine, buy her a diamond ring

SPEAKER:
On his way, Jakey sees a small dark creature
skittering on the river ice
bounding up into the cold air
a weasel
still for a moment
then gone into the trees

SPEAKER:
Alice can't sleep, night after night…

ALICE:
Something's in the wind…

SPEAKER:
She walks down to the river
lights of the town on the other side sparkle on the
water
buoys clang, distant foghorn of a barge in the mist
lights on the far shore go out, one by one

(Vision of ALICE*)*

(Suggested music: Sleepwalk *[Santo and Johnny])*

SPEAKER:
La selva oscura
Midway
Across the orange clouds of sunset
once again seeking their nests in the walls
crows fly home
Jakey buys a bottle of Italian red wine

JAKE:
Lacryma Christi, from the slopes of Vesuvius

Blacktop lined with the houses of working people
through the quiet town to the River Road.
It's Christmas Eve
clear night, stars above
out on the river
buoy bells ring in the mist
A small house, Xmas lights

SPEAKER:
And he knocks
the door opens
and there's Alice
Shakey Jake drops the wine bottle and it shatters at his
feet

ALICE:
You son of a bitch
I thought you were dead
No calls no e-mails
Years of silence
Then one letter
One letter

JAKE:
You never wrote back

ALICE:
Fuck you Jakey
Go re-enlist
let them ship you back to Honduras
Or blow over to the interstate
hold up a cardboard sign
Anywhere, out of this world

JAKE:
I've come a long way, Alice

ALICE:
So have I
You've behaved extremely fucking poorly, Jakey

I don't give a damn about the excuses you're about to
lay on me

JAKE:
Alice…

ALICE:
You could have been in prison, for all I care

JAKE:
I was, sort of…

ALICE:
You're a self centered thoughtless sonofabitch

JAKE:
Alice….

ALICE:
You hearing me, Jakey?

JAKE:
Alice…

ALICE:
What?

JAKE:
Even if you don't love me anymore,
why not just be kind?

ALICE:
Who do you think I am, for God's sake, that I should
be kind to you?
You've been gone, Jakey
You could have found me anytime
I wasn't hiding
I never left, not really
Home after college, broke, confused
signed up for two years on the Navajo rez teaching
second grade
Mornings before dawn I'd drive miles in the dark
to watch the sun color the jagged needle of Shiprock

blood red, then orange and gold
No one out there but me and the sheep
I lived in Echo Park City of the Angels
waiting tables at Delia's Bistro
got hit on by extremely pretty people
then back to college, U W Seattle this time
M F A in studio art
Day I got my degree I packed up my paints and
drawings
moved back home
into my old room
every stuffed animal in its place, even Pinkie
Long nights alone, my parents asleep
I stare at the cracks in the ceiling
tears run down my cheeks don't even know why
Tick tock
Married a local guy with a job
I was pregnant with his child and he said he loved me
The marriage was a lie
He knew it, and it hurt him
there was nothing I could do
It ended three years ago
He never knew who was in bed alongside him
I haven't seen you for ten years, Jakey
You must have been busy
important shit to do

JAKE:
Don't make fun of me
I went where the wind blew me, Alice
taking whatever came my way
I lived in Dallas, Albuquerque, Taos, Eugene Oregon
Columbus Ohio
even down in Mexico dusty seaside town called
Guaymas
I had a room right off the zocalo
drank pulque and tequila

slept it off and did it all over again
till I understood I was trying to kill myself
and came back to the Promised Land
I worked every kind of job till I left or got fired
bookstore clerk dishwasher lawn maintenance truck
driver movie usher
best was the Forest Service
fire lookout tree planting roadwork
always broke stupid lonely
scrawling stuff in notebooks
I numbered those notebooks
twenty-nine and counting
Once I was hitchhiking to somewhere else
Midwinter so damn cold
I went into a farmer's field and stole the shirt off a
scarecrow
Last four years I was in the service
Decided three squares a day and taking orders might
shape me up

ALICE:
You travel? See the world?
Become a man?

JAKE:
Not exactly
Four years in Honduras
protecting the air base
from the mosquitos and the whores and the heat
I'd sooner be dead and in hell with the wicked
than to hear that bugle sound one more time
I never forgot you, Alice

ALICE:
I don't believe you

JAKE:
Not in the U S Army
Not anywhere else

ALICE:
I don't believe you

JAKE:
True anyway, Alice, if you believe it or not
Since I left the service
wherever I was
you never left me
You were there every night in my dreams
Alice, what's wrong?
Alice, stop crying, please
I shouldn't have come back here

ALICE:
That's not it
I'm just…it's not like it was, Jakey
I'm not eighteen years old, not anymore
Let's drink a glass of wine
I've got a bottle of red here somewhere
and then you have to go
Tomorrow's Christmas Day
I need to wrap presents for my son
He's asleep in his room
I'd show him to you but we might wake him
he's four years old

JAKE:
What's his name?

ALICE:
His name's Lucas
I call him Lukey
Lukey-loo
Were you married, Jakey?

JAKE:
I had a girlfriend
A nurse
We lived together for three years

before the army
She worked emergency rooms
car wrecks, heart attacks, gunshot wounds…
her spirit always bright despite the pain
she saw on every shift
She left me for a bald man with a beard who came into
the E R
With his son
Broke his arm playing soccer

ALICE:
You're kidding me?

JAKE:
No
She was a sensible girl, in the end
I was unemployed
didn't love her
and was drinking too much

SPEAKER:
They go outside
two lawnchairs
blue moonlight on the river ice

ALICE:
No accident
All this
What happens
Look up there in the sky, Jakey
All those cold stars

JAKE:
Comanche moon
just enough light for the riders to come steal your
horses
burn your cabin down…
after we stole their land

ALICE:
That moon's beautiful, Jakey

JAKE:
That too

ALICE:
I'm kind of insomniac lately—sleep when I can
I'm used to it—nights don't seem quite as long as they
used to
I've taken in a lot of moonlight down along that river

JAKE:
Alice, you know something?
I was gonna be that kid forever
standing in front of the pizza joint, collar up
one foot tapping a rhythm only I could hear
The leaves turned red while I wasn't looking

ALICE:
They may not be giving away a pony at this party,
Jakey
but there may be dancing just the same

SPEAKER:
And along the River Road comes Santa Claus
right on time
Fifth of Night Train and he drains it, tosses the dead
soldier into the trees
Skinny older gentleman
half-dressed for the part
only the red hat
scraggly white beard

SWEET LUCY:
Yo ho ho, kids
Merry fucking Christmas

JAKE:
Merry fucking Christmas yourself, Santa

ALICE:
Where's the rest of your outfit?

SWEET LUCY:
You know that Children's Cancer Hospital over in
Rapid City
few towns down the river
They hired me, gave me the entire Santa suit
I was gonna go round all the wards tomorrow morning
even hospice where the kids are dying
and give 'em candy canes
I paused at the Solid Gold Gentleman's Club to refresh
myself
When I heard the first rumbles I thought it was
thunder
Then the bar was shaking
boulder the size of a house crashed through the roof
squashed the barmaid flat
I ran for the car, left everything
red suit, candy canes, half a beer on the bar
Helluva Santa
Sweet Lucy, you screwed up bigtime...

ALICE:
Santa, you're crying...

SWEET LUCY:
Doesn't matter anymore
Cancer hospital caught fire
floors collapsed, beds in flames...
a pile of smoking rubble
All those kids are out of their misery

JAKE:
What?

ALICE:
What'd you say?

SWEET LUCY:
That story make you deaf, Alice?

SPEAKER:
A young woman

Raggedy jeans, leather jacket she's painted up in flames
dances out of the dark on the River Road
Face of an angel, ladies and gentlemen
Tender-lipped, delicate, dewy-eyed

SWEET LUCY:
I've been rude
They call me Sweet Lucy
This is my associate, Snake Hips
Snake Hips, say Merry Christmas to the good people

SNAKE HIPS:
Merry fuckin' Christmas, Jakey
Welcome home
I made it from Newport News to this very spot
with a pack of Chesterfields and a box of English
Breakfast tea
Stay outta the bars near the base, Alice
Those sailors can get nasty

ALICE:
Do we know you?

SNAKE HIPS:
You gotta be careful in this life
Anything can happen
If you're in luck you won't die
before you get to Chicago
or El Paso, or here
wherever the fuck we are.
You're looking wicked, Alice
You may be a poor girl, but you got oil wells in your
backyard
You cut down on the drinking?
What's that lipstick you got on?
Flamingo Pink?

ALICE:
Do we know you?

SNAKE HIPS:
We know you
Everyone around here knows Shakey Jake and Alice

JAKE:
Sweet Lucy, maybe you and Mrs. Claus could find
another place to hang
Alice and me
we're having a private conversation

SWEET LUCY:
Don't mind if I do

SNAKE HIPS:
And Sweet Lucy parks his ass in a lawn chair near
Alice and Shakey Jake

SWEET LUCY:
As I was saying
we had a skyblue Lincoln Continental
took that barge for a test drive
Snake Hips neglected to return it to the dealership
We pulled into Rapid City on a balmy evening
and as I previously mentioned
the Solid Gold Gentleman's Club exploded
I flee the screams of the dying, hustle back to the
Lincoln
Snake Hips had been waiting in the car, as she's
underage
Fucking flying fire hydrant shatters the windshield
Then somebody's fridge makes a direct hit on the front
hood,
crushes the damn motor block
The earth trembles under our feet
fiery lava gushes up from cracks in the sidewalk
houses burst into flames
whirlwinds of sparks and ash swirl down the streets
T V sets, stoves, beds, all dance in the wind like
autumn leaves

roofs are flung into the clouds
Red smoke fills the sky

SNAKE HIPS:
Without wings, no one could fly away
The last judgment had come

SWEET LUCY:
Thirty thousand inhabitants of Rapid City were
crushed under the ruins
Snake Hips was gone, no doubt buried
under a ton of concrete
I cried out Snake Hips! Snake Hips!
I sat down on a pile of corpses and wept
Then I saw Snake Hips her own self

SNAKE HIPS:
Stepping delicately through the smoking rubble
going through the pockets of the dead
slipping rings from bloody fingers
We're born in a convulsion of pain, and die in fear and
agony
Where we come from, and where we go, I have no
fucking idea

SWEET LUCY:
The fire burned Sweet Lucy's lungs
The moon of my life is sinking low
Any time now
I'll be doing the dog-paddle on the river between life
and death

SNAKE HIPS:
Sweet Lucy!
That Night Train wine has fogged your powerful mind
You're healthy as a grizzly bear!
A phoenix!
Besides, these kids are not gonna give you any cash
money
They don't have two dimes to rub together

Death and destruction in Rapid City?
Well, life is an uncertain business
Don't worry yourselves
If there's fire on the mountain
lightning in the air
and the river runs red with blood
we can make it across
all four of us
We have been through hell before

JAKE:
What do the two of you want here?

SWEET LUCY:
Want?

SNAKE HIPS:
Want?

SWEET LUCY:
Want?
I want some of that Cadillac Club wine you're drinking
Spodee odee
Nothing for Snake Hips
She's abstemious
nobody at all
Once I'm sufficiently lubricated
I want to see Alice do the Hully Gully, the Shimmy
Cano,
the Stomp Bomppity Bomp, the Mashed Potato!
Spin that Victrola!
Hold on!
Before the dancing, the poetry
I love me some Longfellow—
By the shores of Gitchee Goomee
By the shining Big Sea Water
Stood the wigwam of Nokomis
Daughter of the Moon, Nokomis
Raised the little Hiawatha

Many things Nokomis taught him
Of the stars that shine above us
Showed him Ishkoodah, the comet
Showed the broad white road in heaven
Pathway of the ghosts, the shadows...
I named my daughter Nokomis
She died of a broken heart
Can happen to you if you love enough...

ALICE:
Uh, Sweet Lucy, you're crying again...

SNAKE HIPS:
He does that

ALICE:
I've got a tissue somewhere...

SNAKE HIPS:
Often
It's the suffering of mankind
one piece or another
Makes him tear right up

JAKE:
Hey, I remember you—years ago, under the River
Road Bridge
Aren't you the guy called himself
Clarence Nightingale...

SWEET LUCY:
Nightingale
Indeed I was
I washed myself clean in the Monongahela
flows into the Cumberland, the Ohio, the Mississippi to
the gulf of Mexicoo
I re-baptized myself Sweet Lucy in those American
rivers
I was healed

JAKE:
How can you get healed from a missing leg?

SWEET LUCY:
Snake Hips raised the cash
to purchase me a lovely leg from China

SNAKE HIPS:
Ten thousand green
came U P S
on ice

SWEET LUCY:
Dr Dingaling was ready for Freddie
stuck his scalpel in the lectric pencil sharpener
got that thing attached in half an hour him drunk too

SNAKE HIPS:
I was on my knees outside the operating room
in prayer

ALICE:
Where's Evangeline?

SWEET LUCY:
Evangeline? Got a job in Woolworth's
Some cowboy told her she lit up the candy counter
ended up in a ditch, duct tape over her mouth

ALICE:
That's a nasty story
Is it true?

SWEET LUCY:
It's educational
Keep looking back over your shoulder
you spot Little Sister Death coming up behind you
Maybe you slip aside and let her pass on by
Truth is
Evangeline is risen from the woods
Too kool to be forgotten
Snake Hips is her latest incarnation

Truth is
Everything that needs saying has already been said
Previously

SNAKE HIPS:
But no one was listening

SWEET LUCY:
Happy trails to you, until we meet again
Happy trails to you, keep smilin' until then…
Come along on the Happy Trails!
I got plans to reinvent America!
I'm running for president
Snake Hips'll be First Lady of the Land

SPEAKER:
And as if by some magic trick
Sweet Lucy's Santa hat has disappeared,
and a raccoon skin's in its place

SNAKE HIPS:
Alice, you still got peaches in your tree
You snap the whip, I'll make the trip

SWEET LUCY:
Snake Hips…

SNAKE HIPS:
Let's you and me go spinning
at the Palace of the Czar

SWEET LUCY:
Snake Hips, your clock is ticking, but you got the
wrong time
The hour is upon us
We got business in the USA
speeches on mountaintops
sermons in parking lots
ring golden doorbells
kiss the babies

You two do what you're supposed to do
Time is winding up

SPEAKER:
Suddenly
and with a whoosh
they're gone

JAKE:
Man o man
Those two were something else entirely

ALICE:
Not entirely

JAKE:
What are you talking about?

ALICE:
I think they had good intentions

JAKE:
Toward us, you mean?

ALICE:
That's what I mean
Can you pour me another glass of wine?

JAKE:
And I'll have one myself
Drink up
Alice, what do you make of this floating world?
A thousand years whirl away on the wind, and here
we are
one time
one night

ALICE:
I don't know, Jakey
I truly don't
One time, one night...
Jakey, you remember that party

last year of high school?
In Arnie what's his name's apartment up that alley

JAKE:
You were there?

ALICE:
You brought me

JAKE:
He had an old steamer trunk full of drugs
Regular pharmacy

ALICE:
I don't know what was in that punch
At one point in the evening you took off your pants
ran over to a window dick flapping in the breeze
announced that you were gonna fly
out that fifth floor window
make a U-turn and fly back in again

JAKE:
Did I do it?

ALICE:
You jumped out the window all right—but on your
way back, you lost altitude

JAKE:
Alice! Why didn't you stop me?

ALICE:
I thought you could make it

JAKE:
I remember I was in the hospital for a month
missed graduation
and the prom
You were gonna be my date

ALICE:
You'd be dead if that mattress truck didn't come
rolling by

Angels on your side, Jakey
still are
lead you by the hand

JAKE:
Maybe...

ALICE:
Brought you back here

JAKE:
Maybe I'm a fortunate son after all
So, here we are
All grown up like everyone else
And the party goes on and on
we keep dancing
the hour grows late
And everyone wonders why it isn't
the way they dreamed it
seven years old lie in the grass look up at the stars

ALICE:
I don't know, Jakey
It seems to me there's
nothing to find, nothing to go back to, nothing to
remember
not really
Just this
And it's all right, Jakey
It truly is

JAKE:
You know, I do say I'm sorry, Alice, only a little at a
time
And not always out loud

ALICE:
I'm not sure I'm ready to forgive you yet
Maybe after a few years of kindness
I might consider it...

I'm sorry too, Jakey
I'm sorry too

JAKE:
You play that guitar?

ALICE:
I'm teaching myself
Mostly I sing Lukey lullabies

JAKE:
Sing me one

ALICE:
Don't laugh at me
Here goes…
(Sings)
Little birdy, little birdy, what makes you fly so high
It's because I am a birdy, and I'm not afraid to die
Little birdy, little birdy, come sing me your song
I've a short time to be here with you, and a long time to
   be gone
I've a short time to be here with you, and a long time to
   be gone
You like it?

JAKE:
Yeah I like it
I could listen to you sing it forever

ALICE:
Now you're laughing at me

JAKE:
No, I'm not
I'm telling you the truth

ALICE:
You know something?
My garden's all overgrown
I neglected it in the fall
And now the zucchini rot on the vine

Maybe I can salvage some seeds
Dry them out for next season...
I did put in five raspberry bushes last summer
You stick around till spring, you can have some

I shouldn't be talking so much to you
I shouldn't be drinking this wine
I've got to wrap this for the morning...

SPEAKER:
And Jakey watches her the way he used to
As she carefully wraps a Christmas gift for her child
She ties the silver ribbon in a bow
Brushes the hair away from her eyes

ALICE:
You're really drunk, Jakey
Aren't you?

JAKE:
Alice, I may have had a little wine
but I'm...

ALICE:
Drunk or sober, I don't care
I've been waiting years for someone to look at me
the way you're looking at me now

SPEAKER:
Alice drinks some more wine
turns on the radio
finds that station she likes...

ALICE:
Are you religious, Jakey? A religious man?

JAKE:
Why you asking me that, Alice?

ALICE:
I don't know
Sometimes I go to Saint Genevieve's in town
once Lukey's at his playgroup in the morning

doors are always open
quiet
No one else is ever there

JAKE:
I don't go to church, if that's what you mean

ALICE:
You know what I mean

JAKE:
Yes I do
I always had those feelings
And that hellhole in Honduras let me know for sure
You know something?
I don't discriminate
I'm a Taoist Islamic Christian Jew
with a helluva lot of Buddhist mixed up in there

SPEAKER:
And Alice turns up the music
The night may be dark and the road may be long
Right now, this moment, it doesn't matter at all

(Vision of JAKE *and* ALICE*)*

(Suggested music: Bring It On Home *[Sam Cooke])*

SPEAKER:
A slow number
And Alice dances
Jake watches her
And she holds out her hand
They dance round Alice's living room
in the American night
As below, so above
the stars move in their courses…
And the dance is done

JAKE:
You asked me something long ago, Alice

ALICE:
What did I ask you?

JAKE:
You asked if I'd remember you on my deathbed
I didn't know the answer back then
Sure as flesh moves over bones
If you're a thousand miles away
or sitting by my side
or already in your grave
You'll be with me on my deathbed

SPEAKER:
And they hold each other

JAKE:
I can taste your tears
This love will burn us up
Nothing left but ashes

ALICE:
It's all right, Jakey
Some things are worth dying for

(Lights shift to hold this final image.)

(Scene out)

III. AT THE BONE ORCHARD

SPEAKER:
Years later
Alice's house
on the River Road
Springtime
Night

SPEAKER:
They stand in the front doorway, Jakey and Alice

JAKE:
Is that something moving out there?

ALICE:
Hard to tell, could be a deer

JAKE:
Or a tree in the wind

ALICE:
There's a full moon
Let's walk down to the river

SPEAKER:
Alice and Jake
down the path to the riverside
Holding hands
Her once blonde hair is gray
tied up in a long ponytail
down her back

JAKE:
You know something, Alice?

ALICE:
What's that, Jakey?

JAKE:
Few weeks ago I saw a boy
alone in a rowboat on the river
riding the current downstream
pulling like mad on the oars
spray flying all around him
laughing and laughing

ALICE:
Who was he?

JAKE:
No idea.
I looked away a moment, and when I turned back to
the river
The boat was gone

ALICE:
Sky's so clear, a million stars
I never told anyone this, Jakey
One time, years ago, I couldn't sleep
came down here in the dark
first thin light rising in the east
In that morning stillness I heard something
like someone calling to me from a great distance
a sound like a promise
Then the first sunlight hit the tops of the trees—a
blossoming
I never felt so fortunate
just to be here

SPEAKER:
They reach a clearing by the riverside
Jake reaches into his pocket, then spreads out his palm

JAKE:
Look what I found this morning in the garden
shell of a cricket, paper-thin, empty
nothing left inside
sang itself utterly away

SPEAKER:
Across the river a town strung out along shore
lights along the streets and in the warm living rooms
people laughing and weeping
arguing screwing driving cars
getting sick getting well
counting their money watching T V
pissing and shitting
giving birth dying
talking on cell phones roller skating eating
fast asleep
a faire field full of folk trying to love one another
going about their business

JAKE:
Down on the corner
Scrapper Blackwell and Yank Rachell—old men now
those same folding chairs in front of the liquor store
Old Harmony Silvertone and a mandolin, voices soft
a little tune in the night...
Don't the moon look lonesome, setting down in the
west
don't the moon look lonesome, setting in the west
of all these good looking women, I love you the best...

SPEAKER:
Alice turns to Jake
rises up on her toes
kisses him lightly on the lips
Jakey's face floats like a dream in front of her...

*****

SPEAKER:
Some months later
a bed, a chair, an I V on a stand
Jakey's dying

He lies on his deathbed, saying something
Alice puts her ear close to his mouth

ALICE:
Jakey, I can't hear you
Louder if you can, Jakey

JAKE:
I should have robbed a bank built you a mansion Alice
on a hill somewhere

ALICE:
I don't want a mansion, Jakey, I never did

JAKE:
That's what you always say…
Alice, no one will remember
who I was
all the people, colors, sounds, moments I loved
who I was
what I told myself in those notebooks

ALICE:
I won't forget you, Jakey

JAKE:
You know what, Alice?
It's okay
It really is

ALICE:
Lucas called
you were sleeping and I didn't want to wake you
He sends his love
He's so sorry he can't be with you

JAKE:
I like hearing that
Tell him to do what he needs to do
get here if he can
I want a drink—bourbon over ice
a straw so I won't spill

ALICE:
Doctor says that's not a good idea

JAKE:
Alice, don't be foolish
I'm dying

SPEAKER #1:
She pours the drink, finds a straw
brings it over

JAKE:
Once I was at a railroad crossing, Alice

nighttime warning bell rings red lights flash
and I saw a young girl in a summer dress
waiting for the train to pass
lit in the oncoming headlight
her dress flying around her in the blowby of the train's
passing
I saw the taillights on the caboose
grow smaller and the train was gone
the girl was gone
And there was an old hobo alongside me
Eyes like burning coals
Well, he says
another little miracle
Now ain't that something...

ALICE:
What are you trying to tell me, Jakey?

JAKE:
I don't know
Just a story
I'm not yet weary of this world, Alice
of seeing your face
I can't die
Who's gonna shoe your pretty little foot,
who's gonna glove your hand
who's gonna kiss your red ruby lips
when I'm in that promised land?
I wouldn't have missed this life
Not for anything...
We're never at the wheel
Not really
not even in the Coupe de Ville
Passengers

Tell you a secret, Alice
I've been in heaven for days...

ALICE:
It's the drugs they've got you taking, Jakey
for the pain

JAKE:
You're here with me
In heaven
crows return to their nests at twilight
you can hear the stream
flowing over the rocks
just like the world I left behind
Sound of your voice
Just as it was below
Alice, I'm cold

SPEAKER:
And she tucks up his covers
straightens the pillow under his head

ALICE:
I'll turn the heat up, be right back

SPEAKER:
And Alice is gone
Blow the mournful sax-o-phone!
Beat the goatskin drum!
Dig his grave with a silver spade…

JAKE:
I can't see you but I know you're there

SPEAKER #1:
And a familiar young woman appears…

LITTLE SISTER:
Is this better?

JAKE:
I can see you now
Are you who I think you are?

LITTLE SISTER:
I don't know who you think I am, Shakey-Jakey
I'm Little Sister
I spin the wheel of your life
My job
You like this look? College girl
I'm a theater major

JAKE:
Who sent you?

LITTLE SISTER:
No one sends me anywhere
That's bullshit
It's totally my call

JAKE:
You remind me of someone

LITTLE SISTER:
Everyone says that about me

JAKE:
Someone I met long ago

LITTLE SISTER:
Doesn't surprise me, Jake
I get around
You know something, Mr Shakey-Jakey?
Down on the riverbank
in the dark of his burrow
an old weasel lies dying
His breathing is ragged
and he no longer has the strength to move
Blood on his jaws
Last kill

By the way, can you give me a ride into town?
You still got that ragtop?
Coupe de Ville Cadillac, Coup de Ville

JAKE:
That car's gone

LITTLE SISTER:
Eight ball suicide knob on the steering wheel?

JAKE:
Gone long ago

LITTLE SISTER:
Funny
Its right outside

JAKE:
Impossible
You're lying to me

LITTLE SISTER:
I don't lie to anyone
Not ever
Take a look

SPEAKER:
And Little Sister opens the curtains

JAKE:
Son of a bitch
There she is
She's shining
New paint job?

LITTLE SISTER:
Un uh, the original candyapple red
I waxed it

JAKE:
Beautiful job

LITTLE SISTER:
Thank you
So
I have other appointments
Gimme a ride downtown

JAKE:
I can't drive, Little Sister
I can't even stand up
Maybe Alice can...

SPEAKER #1:
And Alice is there
and she nods to Little Sister
No surprise

LITTLE SISTER:
Alice, I was certain I'd see you here
I'm Little Sister

ALICE:
I know who you are

LITTLE SISTER:
I brought you and Jakey a poem, comes before the dancing
Love me some Longfellow
On the shore stood Hiawatha,
Launched his birch canoe for sailing,
Westward, westward Hiawatha
Sailed into the dusk of evening

Thus departed Hiawatha,
To the Islands of the Blessed,
To the Land of the Hereafter...

ALICE:
Stop that, please

LITTLE SISTER:
Alice, where's your feeling for American verse?

ALICE:
Can't you see Jakey's trying to rest?

LITTLE SISTER:
He's not trying to rest, Alice
He's trying to die

It's a good day for it
Horse in the valley, who's gonna ride him?
Always the same trip, Alice, tears at the end of it
You two did very well, considering

ALICE:
Considering what?

LITTLE SISTER:
How it is
on this tiny clod of dirt
spinning through space
Changed some rainwater into wine after all, Angel
Alice

JAKE:
Tell me, Little Sister
before my flesh and spirit fused into one, who was I?
who will I be when they come apart in the grave?

LITTLE SISTER:
I don't know anything about those things, Jakey
One world at a time

JAKE:
I remember you now, Little Sister
Snake Hips

LITTLE SISTER:
I've been called that

JAKE:
And Evangeline
Clarence? Sweet Lucy?

LITTLE SISTER:
He's busy, or he would have come around to see you
one more time
I'm going now, Jakey
Let you and Alice be alone with each other
I'm taking your car
you won't need it anymore

I'll see you again Jakey
home at last
Down this road goes no one
It's all light

SPEAKER:
And Little Sister's gone
Alice and Shakey-Jake

ALICE:
Before you came back to me
I'd sit by the river and swear I would not move from
watching the water until you came back
Into my heart
Into my bed
Or until the frost came and turned my hair white
Now it has
Two old lies, Jakey
and here's the truth
Time doesn't pass
Love doesn't fade
When we come round again
I want you to find me
love me through another lifetime
no matter what I've become in the next life
the next world
on and on
as long as the wheel turns

JAKE:
Alice, if you're a tree in the forest
or a drop of water in the river
or a spirit in the air
I'll find you

SPEAKER:
Jakey cries out
as something inside him breaks at last

JAKE:
Here comes Death
To me
Only a child…

SPEAKER:
Alice takes Jakey in her arms
Her lips to his
Her tears on his cheek

******

SPEAKER:
Winter
She's alone
is Alice

(Vision of ALICE*)*

(Suggested music: Graceful Ghost Rag *[Eugene Barban])*

ALICE:
I always thought to pick you a bouquet of wildflowers
I never got around to it
and here I am
laying wildflowers
on your grave
I hope you like them
I'm your girl, Jakey
Now and forever
I'm your girl
Don't know where I'm going, but I know I've been
there before
Pray for us, for me and Jakey
and pray for each other as this bright world sails on
through the fierce emptiness
the spirits of all the dead in its starry wake

SPEAKER:
Snow falls
gathers in the valleys and on the peaks
on the streets of towns and cities
dissolves into the broad Atlantic sea
Alice brushes it out of her hair
She reaches down to the snow on Jakey's grave
cups some to her mouth
Sweet and cold
The world in all its beauty cannot comfort her
Alice dies of loneliness
And after some years, no one will remember
Shakey Jake and Alice
They lie next to each other in their quiet graves
in the sun and in the rain
The wind blows over them
for evermore

(ALICE *and* JAKE *appear, next to each other.*)

(*Lights shift to hold this final image.*)

(*Scene out*)

END OF PLAY

If anyone should ask you
Who it was that sang this song
Tell 'em it was Len Jenkin
He was a longtime here
He'll be a longtime gone